1880

French engineer Gustave Eiffel designs the supporting iron framework for Liberty's copper skin.

W9-AVS-988

October 28–November 1, 1886

The statue is unveiled to the public on its pedestal on Bedloe's Island in New York. There are parades, fireworks, and speeches.

December 1884

The statue is taken apart again and shipped to New York.

1884

The statue is finished in Paris and becomes a big tourist attraction.

April 22, 1886

The concrete and stone pedestal for the statue is finally completed.

Lady Liberty's Journey

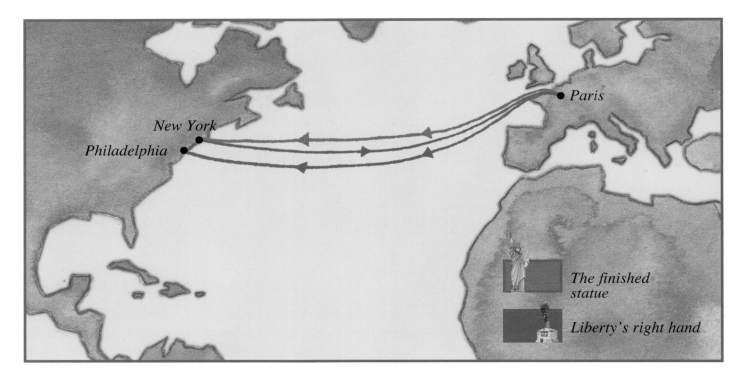

New York
Philadelphia
Paris

The finished statue

Liberty's right hand

Before it even had legs or feet, the Statue of Liberty did an impressive amount of traveling! When the torch-holding right hand of the statue was first finished, it was shipped across the Atlantic Ocean to Philadelphia, Pennsylvania, for the city's Centennial Exhibition, in 1876, before moving on to Madison Square in New York. Thousands of people paid to climb inside it and admire the view.

After a six-year trip abroad, Liberty's right hand was returned to France in 1882. Once it arrived back in Paris, it was attached to the rest of the statue, which had been built during its absence. The completed Statue of Liberty was put on display in Paris before being shipped in pieces to its final resting place: Bedloe's Island in New York, which is now known as Liberty Island.

MCFL Distribution Center Children's
J 974.7 Malam
You wouldn't want to be a worker
31111038081277

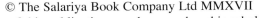

Author:
John Malam studied ancient history and archeology at the University of Birmingham, England. After that he worked as an archeologist at the Ironbridge Gorge Museum in Shropshire. He is now an author specializing in nonfiction books for children. He lives in Cheshire, England, with his wife and their two children.

Artist:
David Antram was born in Brighton, England, in 1958. He studied at Eastbourne College of Art and then worked in advertising for 15 years before becoming a full-time artist. He has illustrated many children's nonfiction books.

Series creator:
David Salariya was born in Dundee, Scotland. He has illustrated a wide range of books and has created and designed many new series for publishers in the UK and overseas. David established The Salariya Book Company in 1989. He lives in Brighton with his wife, illustrator Shirley Willis, and their son, Jonathan.

Editor: **Stephen Haynes**

Editorial Assistant: **Mark Williams**

© The Salariya Book Company Ltd MMXVII
No part of this publication may be reproduced in whole or in part, or stored in a retrieval system, or transmitted in any form or by any means, electronic, mechanical, photocopying, recording, or otherwise, without written permission of the publisher. For information regarding permission, write to the copyright holder.

Published in Great Britain in 2017 by
The Salariya Book Company Ltd
25 Marlborough Place, Brighton BN1 1UB

ISBN-13: 978-0-531-23833-2 (lib. bdg.) 978-0-531-23155-5 (pbk.)

All rights reserved.
Published in 2017 in the United States
by Franklin Watts
An imprint of Scholastic Inc.

A CIP catalog record for this book is available from the Library of Congress.

Printed and bound in China.
Printed on paper from sustainable sources.

1 2 3 4 5 6 7 8 9 10 R 26 25 24 23 22 21 20 19 18 17

SCHOLASTIC, FRANKLIN WATTS, and associated logos are trademarks and/or registered trademarks of Scholastic Inc.

This book is sold subject to the conditions that it shall not, by way of trade or otherwise, be lent, resold, hired out, or otherwise circulated without the publisher's prior consent in any form or binding or cover other than that in which it is published and without similar condition being imposed on the subsequent purchaser.

PAPER FROM
SUSTAINABLE
FORESTS

You Wouldn't Want to Be a Worker on the Statue of Liberty!

Written by
John Malam

Illustrated by
David Antram

Created and designed by
David Salariya

A Monument You'd Rather Not Build

Franklin Watts®
An Imprint of Scholastic Inc.

Contents

Introduction

The year is 1871, and you are in Paris, the capital of France. You work as a humble assistant to Frédéric Auguste Bartholdi, a sculptor who's becoming quite well known. He's been invited to meet with Édouard de Laboulaye, a politician who loves the United States of America. It won't be the first time that Bartholdi has met him.

Six years ago, at a dinner party in 1865, Laboulaye told Bartholdi that he wanted to give a present to the United States from the people of France. Laboulaye thought it would be a good idea to give a statue to America. He said it would be a symbol of friendship between the two countries. But for years, nothing came of the idea.

Now, however, Bartholdi thinks that plans for the statue might really go ahead. If so, Bartholdi wants to be the statue's sculptor— and that will mean a lot of hard, sometimes dangerous work for you. *Bonne chance!* (Good luck!)

Vivent nos républiques!

(Long live our republics!)

A Statue? A Big Idea Is Born

How big? The man must be mad!

Édouard de Laboulaye has invited several important men to his house. He tells them about his idea of giving a statue to the people of America, and says it has to be ready in five years' time, by 1876. Why then? Because that's when the United States will be celebrating its 100th birthday. It became an independent country in 1776, and the statue will be a special birthday present.

Laboulaye points to the figure of Liberty on the great seal of France. He wants to give the Americans their own Liberty statue—a monument to freedom. He has even thought of a name for it—a rather long one. As for the design of the statue, Bartholdi shocks everyone when he says he wants to build a colossus—a giant statue. You'll have your work cut out for you!

Inspiration

ALL TALK? Laboulaye first mentioned the idea at an earlier dinner party in 1865— the last year of the American Civil War. But so far nothing has been done about it.

LIBERTAS AND LIBERTY. Bartholdi didn't just make up the design out of his own head. Other artists before him had imagined how Liberty might look (see opposite page).

1. ROMAN COINS were often stamped with *Libertas*, the goddess of freedom.

2. GREAT SEAL. Liberty is shown on the seal of the French Republic.

3. PAINTING. *The Republic Enlightening the World* (1848) by French artist A. L. Janet-Lange.

Bon Voyage! Off to America

Lighthouse

EGYPT. In 1867 Bartholdi designed a giant lighthouse for Suez, Egypt. It was never built, but his design gave him ideas for the Statue of Liberty.

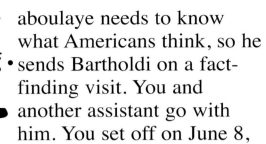

Laboulaye needs to know what Americans think, so he sends Bartholdi on a fact-finding visit. You and another assistant go with him. You set off on June 8, 1871, and 13 uncomfortable days later your ship sails into New York Harbor. It passes Bedloe's Island, and Bartholdi thinks this would be a good place to put the statue. You spend the next three months traveling around the United States trying to drum up support, but Americans just aren't interested in the project. You really wish you'd stayed at home!

Bartholdi on Tour

THE BIG CITY. Bartholdi explores New York City, which he's heard so much about.

THE PRESIDENT. He meets Ulysses S. Grant, president of the United States.

I enjoyed your "Hiawatha."

THE POET. He also meets Henry Wadsworth Longfellow, America's most famous living poet.

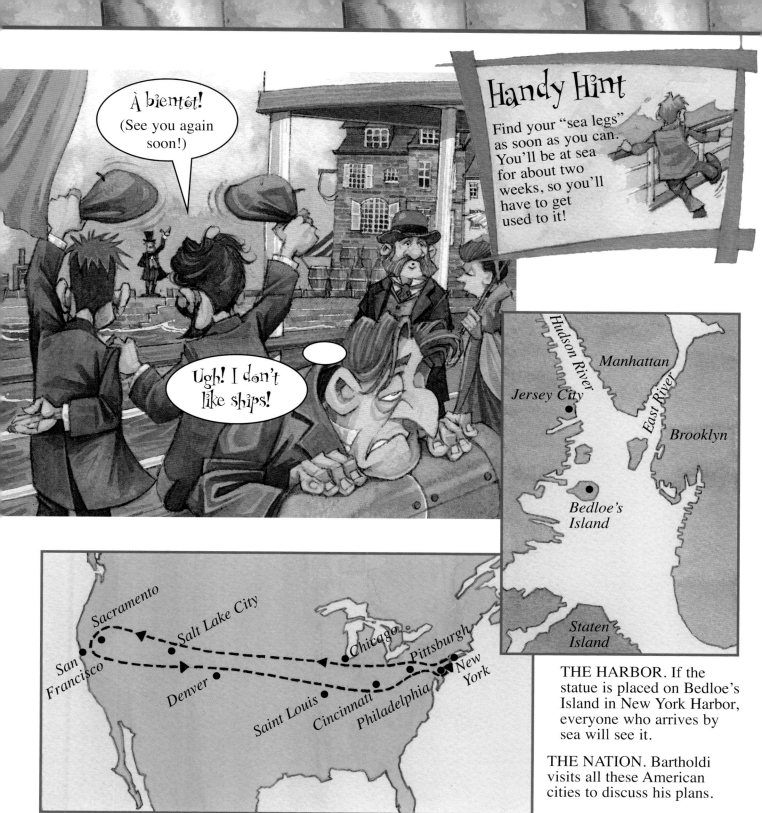

À bientôt!
(See you again soon!)

Ugh! I don't like ships!

Handy Hint

Find your "sea legs" as soon as you can. You'll be at sea for about two weeks, so you'll have to get used to it!

THE HARBOR. If the statue is placed on Bedloe's Island in New York Harbor, everyone who arrives by sea will see it.

THE NATION. Bartholdi visits all these American cities to discuss his plans.

A Giantess! Designing Liberty

My arm is killing me.

Phrygian cap

Back in Paris, Bartholdi makes sketches and models of how Liberty might look. It's your job to help him work out his ideas, and sometimes you feel a bit silly...

He plans to make the statue about 148 feet (45 m) high. It's meant to represent freedom, so he adds some symbols of freedom. He tries a Phrygian cap—a hat worn in Roman times by ex-slaves who had gained their freedom. But not everyone would recognize that symbol, so he changes the cap to a crown with rays. He likes the idea of Liberty holding a broken chain—everyone knows that is a sign of freedom. But he changes that, too. It's so hard working with artists— they're never satisfied!

ROUGH IDEAS. These are some of the ideas that Bartholdi tries out before he settles on the final design.

Handy Hint

Freeze! Do not forget your pose. Monsieur Bartholdi will ask you to stand in this exact position again and again and again!

Can't you keep your arm still?

Model Mother?

MADAME BARTHOLDI. Some say that Bartholdi's mother, Charlotte, was the model for Liberty's face.

That's my boy!

11

Into the Mine! A Visit to Norway

Copper Saint

A GIANT hollow statue made of copper already exists. It was made in Italy in 1697 and is a statue of St. Charles Borromeo.

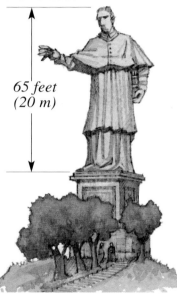

65 feet
(20 m)

The statue is far too big to be made from stone or solid metal. Bartholdi has decided to make it from thin sheets of copper, attached to an iron frame. Even though it will be hollow, Liberty will still need 100 tons of pure copper. There is only one place to get it—the copper mines at Vigsnes in Norway.

It's your job to go there and make sure that only the best copper is sent to Paris. You have to go into the mine and see the lumps of copper ore dug out of the rock. Then you watch as the ore is crushed and heated to produce liquid copper. It's hot, dangerous work—the copper fumes contain arsenic and other deadly poisons.

PURE COPPER. A rich vein of copper was discovered at Vigsnes in 1865. By the 1870s, that mine is the leading producer of copper in Europe.

Why Copper?

SOFT. Copper can be beaten into shape more easily than other metals.

WILL NOT CRACK. Copper can be bent without cracking.

WILL NOT RUST. Iron rusts (left), but copper doesn't (right).

SELF-PROTECTING. Copper develops a protective greenish patina.

Who Pays?

The money for the statue comes from:

THE FRANCO-AMERICAN UNION, a fundraising group set up by Laboulaye.

PEOPLE OF FRANCE. Towns collect people's money and send it off.

FRENCH BUSINESS PEOPLE. One man has sent 64 tons of copper.

SOUVENIRS. 200 mini statues are sold at 1,000 francs ($350) each.

Plastered! Liberty Takes Shape

You thought the copper mines in Norway were bad enough, but now you're choking in plaster dust! At the workshop of Gaget, Gauthier & Co. in Paris, the air is full of it. Here a full-size model of Liberty is taking shape, bit by bit. Each piece starts off as a small clay model. Then it's over to you to measure it. By doubling the measurements you make a model twice the size. You continue to multiply the measurements, creating bigger and bigger models. You've got to take thousands of accurate measurements. The full-size pieces, made of wood, then have to be covered in plaster.

PIECE BY PIECE. Bartholdi divides the statue into about 310 sections; it takes 38 pieces to make the right hand and torch. Measurements have to be taken at many different points. Each section needs about 9,000 measurements, which can then be scaled up to make full-size models. This scaling-up technique is called "pointing up."

Starting Small

1. SCALE MODEL. The maquette (as sculptors call it) is made from clay. It's one-sixteenth the size of the actual statue.

2. SECTION. A larger model is made of each part—one-quarter the size of the actual statue.

3. ACTUAL SIZE. Each section is scaled up to the size it will really be.

Strings called plumb lines are used as a guide for measuring. A metal weight makes the string hang exactly vertical.

Plumb line

Caliper

15

Molded! Liberty in Wood

As if the plastering wasn't hard enough, the next job is really tricky. Now you have to shape huge wooden molds that fit exactly onto the outside of each plaster section. The shapes are complicated, and it takes skill to make the molds fit around them. You can't leave any gaps between the wood and the plaster, or the copper sheets won't fit together once they've been beaten into shape. Remember the carpenter's golden rule: measure twice, cut once.

Careful! No gaps, please.

TOOLS OF THE TRADE. A carpenter's toolbox contains his planes for smoothing, braces and bits for drilling holes, chisels for cutting, and a carpenter's square for marking out right angles.

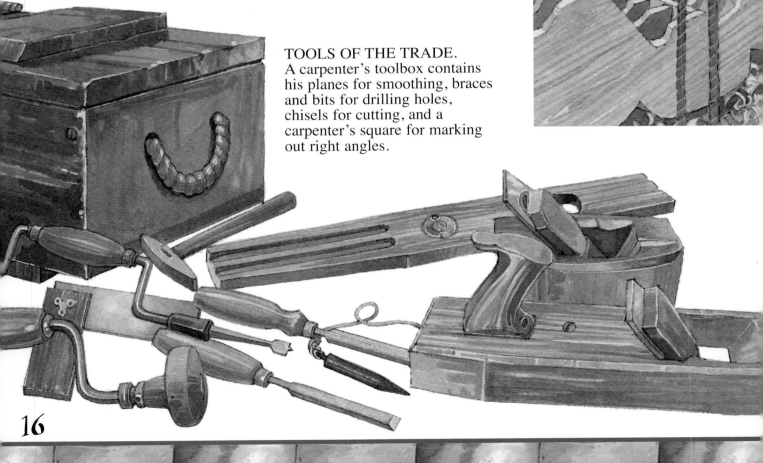

I'm doing my best, sir!

Handy Hint

Watch the chisel, not the mallet! If you take your eyes off it for a second, you'll be sorry...

!*%$*!!

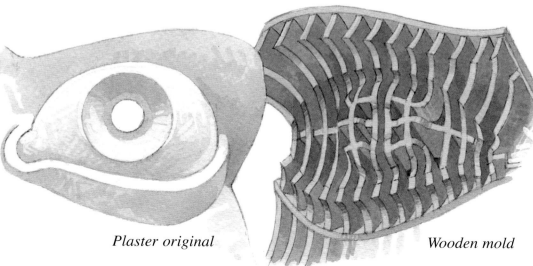

TIGHT FIT. Here's part of the mold for one of Liberty's eyes. It's called a "negative impression"— an inside-out version of the plaster original.

Plaster original

Wooden mold

17

Hammered! Liberty's Copper Skin

The wooden molds are taken into the fabrication room, which is where Liberty's copper skin is knocked into shape. Spend too long in here, and you could easily go deaf. Flat sheets of copper are laid onto each mold. They're placed on the side of the mold that was shaped to fit around the plaster section. The sheets are then beaten with hammers until they are pressed and bent into the shape of the mold. The beaten copper sheets are now the exact shapes needed for the statue—you hope!

For complicated shapes, the copper must be heated in a forge until it is soft—which means more of those dangerous fumes.

When you're drilling metal, watch out for the sharp metal shavings that come out of the hole. If a piece gets in your eye, you could be blinded.

Right-Hand Men

HOLES. Endless rows of holes have to be drilled into the edges of the finished sheets of copper. These holes are for the rivets that will join the sheets together. More rivets will hold the copper sheets to the armature (right).

Handy Hint

The copper sheets that have been in the forge will be too hot to handle! Wear gloves so you don't burn your fingers.

Been.

Been who?

Knock Knock!

Been knocking so long, my head hurts!

Armature

Rivet

BIG HAND. Here's the right hand after all the molded copper pieces have been joined together like a three-dimensional jigsaw puzzle. The torch is 21 feet (6.4 m) tall.

ARMATURE. The statue's armature, or "skeleton," is a network of iron bars fitted to the insides of the copper sheets. The sheets are attached to the bars with rivets and bolts.

19

Torch Bearer! Hand Across the Sea

Hand on Tour

1876: PHILADELPHIA.
Liberty's right hand and torch are displayed at the Philadelphia Centennial Exhibition. Thousands of people pay to climb inside.

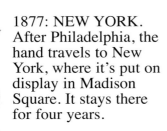

1877: NEW YORK.
After Philadelphia, the hand travels to New York, where it's put on display in Madison Square. It stays there for four years.

It's now 1876, but Liberty isn't ready for America's 100th-birthday party! All that's finished is the right hand. It'll have to do, so it's shipped over from France to the United States. The hand is exhibited in Philadelphia before moving to New York. It's your second visit to America, and you and Bartholdi have got a lot to do. Last time you came here, most people were not interested—but you're hoping the giant hand will change their minds. You've got to convince them to raise money for the massive pedestal that Liberty will stand on—or else the whole project could fail.

Meanwhile, Back in Paris...

1878: HEAD AND SHOULDERS. Liberty's head and shoulders are completed. They're displayed at the Universal Exposition in Paris. Inside is a winding staircase, and visitors pay to climb up to the windows in the crown.

1880: IRON SKELETON. French engineer Gustave Eiffel (he'll be famous one day for his tower) designs the iron framework or armature that will support Liberty's copper skin.

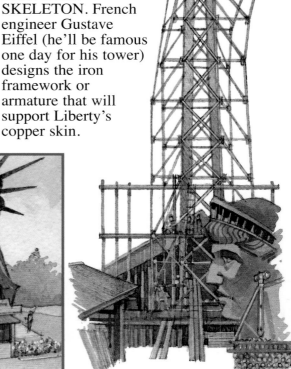

Handy Hint

Your job depends on raising enough money to finish the statue. Help sell tickets for people to climb up the stairs inside the arm.

It wasn't this color in Paris.

Copper quickly tarnishes. One day Liberty will be green!

1882: HANDED BACK. After being in the United States for six years, Liberty's right hand is shipped back to France, so it can be joined to the rest of the statue.

1884: ABOVE THE ROOFTOPS. Liberty is finished! The statue is fully assembled and towers over the buildings of Paris. Crowds of Parisians come to look.

On a Pedestal! Liberty's Island Home

STAR FORT. Fort Wood is an old army fort on Bedloe's Island. Built in 1811, it is shaped like a star with eleven points. Liberty's pedestal will go here.

HOSPITAL. In 1861, during the American Civil War, Fort Wood was used as a hospital for sick and wounded Confederate prisoners. Also, travelers who arrived in America with contagious diseases were kept on the island until they recovered.

I n 1877 the government of the United States agrees that Liberty can be put up on Bedloe's Island. The giant statue will stand in the center of an old fort, on a concrete and stone pedestal built by American architect Richard Morris Hunt. This is the good news. The bad news is that the project to build the pedestal keeps running out of money, and each time that happens, the work has to stop. You've just got to stay calm and hope that enough money will be raised to finish building the base. If that doesn't happen, all your hard work will have been for nothing.

1884: Laying the Cornerstone

SILVER TROWEL. The mortar is spread with a ceremonial trowel.

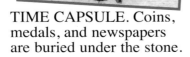

TIME CAPSULE. Coins, medals, and newspapers are buried under the stone.

SQUARE AND TRUE. After the stone has been positioned, it's checked to make sure it's perfectly level.

AND FINALLY: Wheat, wine, and oil are sprinkled over the stone. They symbolize abundance, joy, and peace.

The base will soon be ready.

Handy Hint

Heads up! There have been no accidents during the building of the pedestal, so let's keep it that way.

It had better be!

The pedestal and foundation are almost exactly the same height as the statue itself. The height from the foundation to the tip of the flame will be 305 feet (93 m).

Possible Pedestals

ROUGH IDEAS. Bartholdi came up with several ideas for the pedestal. He thought Liberty could stand on a pyramid-shaped base or on top of a tall tower. Neither idea was used.

Pyramid

Tower

Shipped! Liberty to America

In December 1884, the time comes for Liberty to begin her voyage to America. In Paris, the giant statue is taken apart and the pieces are packed into 214 crates, all clearly numbered. A train takes them to the port of Rouen, where it takes 17 days to load the heavy boxes onto a ship. It's not all plain sailing! The crossing is a slow and stormy one. In New York, some of the crates are damaged when they're unloaded. But worst of all, the pedestal still isn't ready! The crates have to go into storage—and that costs money.

Sixty-five...

Are they putting me on?

Coast to Coast

ATLANTIC CROSSING. The crates are loaded onto the French steamship *Isère*. It sails from Rouen on May 21, 1885, and reaches New York 28 days later.

STORMY WEATHER. The first part of the crossing is stormy and the ship uses up most of its coal. It has to stop at the Azores Islands to refuel.

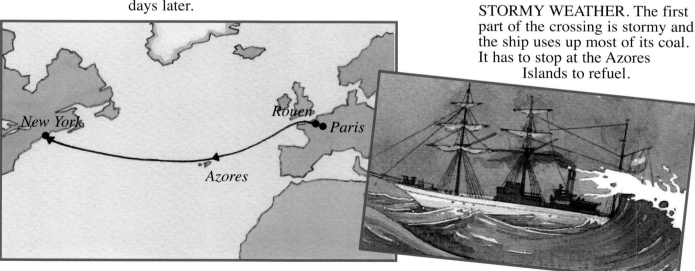

New York · *Rouen* · *Paris* · *Azores*

STACK 'EM HIGH. The crates are stacked on Bedloe's Island, where they will remain almost a year until the pedestal is ready.

PEDESTAL FINISHED. The campaign to raise funds for the pedestal is helped by newspaper owner Joseph Pulitzer. Readers of his paper give $102,000. On April 22, 1886, as the last block of stone is put in place for the pedestal, workers throw silver coins into the mortar. At last it is time for Liberty to take her place.

Standing Tall! Liberty Rising

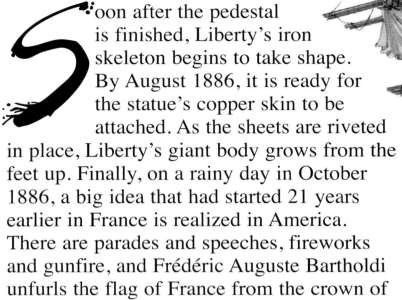

Putting it All Together

UNPACKED. Liberty's copper sheets are taken from their packing crates. Each piece is labeled so the Americans know where to fit them.

REPAIRS. Some pieces are found to be damaged and have to be repaired.

Soon after the pedestal is finished, Liberty's iron skeleton begins to take shape. By August 1886, it is ready for the statue's copper skin to be attached. As the sheets are riveted in place, Liberty's giant body grows from the feet up. Finally, on a rainy day in October 1886, a big idea that had started 21 years earlier in France is realized in America. There are parades and speeches, fireworks and gunfire, and Frédéric Auguste Bartholdi unfurls the flag of France from the crown of the Statue of Liberty.

Will it fit?

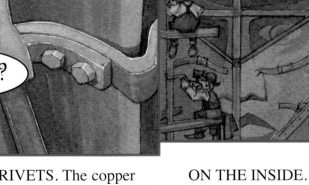

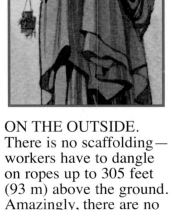

RIVETS. The copper sheets have to be riveted to Eiffel's armature by hand—a noisy, back-breaking job. The first two rivets are named "Bartholdi" and "Pulitzer"!

ON THE INSIDE. Riveters have to climb up the iron armature inside the statue. When the sun shines on the copper, it gets unbearably hot inside.

ON THE OUTSIDE. There is no scaffolding—workers have to dangle on ropes up to 305 feet (93 m) above the ground. Amazingly, there are no serious accidents.

Pardon?

Handy Hint

Keep checking the drawings to make sure you know where all the 300-plus pieces of copper fit.

THE BIG DAY. On October 28, 1886, Bartholdi drapes a French flag from Liberty's crown. At last the giant statue is finished!

I don't like heights, but I'm putting a brave face on it.

It's about time!

Colossus! Liberty Fact File

It didn't take long for the Statue of Liberty to become world-famous. Staring out to sea in the direction of Europe, she soon became a symbol of the United States. In the late 1800s and early 1900s, thousands of people left Europe to begin new lives across the Atlantic. The light from Liberty's torch was a welcoming sight as their ships sailed into New York Harbor.

AT THE TOP. Twelve people at a time could stand in the torch gallery (now closed).

ALL THE SEVENS. The crown, or nimbus, has seven rays—one for each continent.

STAIRCASE. The spiral staircase inside the statue and pedestal has 354 steps.

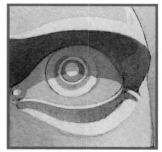

EYES WIDE OPEN. Each eye is 2ft 6in (76 cm) wide.

WORLD'S TALLEST. In 1886, the Statue of Liberty was said to be the world's tallest monument.

Note: Only the tops of the monuments are shown here.

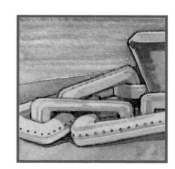

CHAINS. Broken chains representing freedom lie at Liberty's right foot.

1 Victory Monument, New Delhi, India
2 Tower of San Martino, near Sirmione, Italy
3 Hercules Monument, Kassel, Germany
4 Battle Monument, Bennington, Vermont
5 Victory Monument, Berlin, Germany
6 War Monument, Indianapolis, Indiana

7 Emperor Wilhelm Monument, Kyffhäuser Mountain, Germany
8 Garfield Memorial, Cleveland, Ohio
9 Scheldt Freedom Monument, Antwerp, Belgium
10 Wellington Obelisk, Dublin, Ireland

LONG NOSE. Liberty's nose measures 4 feet, 6 inches (137 cm) long.

TABLET. The date is July 4, 1776—the date of the Declaration of Independence.

SECRET ENTRANCE. There's a doorway in the sole of the right foot.

POEM. Emma Lazarus's poem about the statue, "The New Colossus," is engraved on a bronze plaque inside Liberty's pedestal. The most famous lines are: "Give me your tired, your poor / Your huddled masses yearning to breathe free"—a reference to immigrants from Europe coming to live in the United States.

TORCH. On November 1, 1886, lights inside the torch were switched on and Liberty became a lighthouse. A new torch was fitted in 1986. On a windy day the torch can sway as much as 5 inches (13 cm).

NAME CHANGE. In 1956, Bedloe's Island was officially renamed Liberty Island.

Glossary

Armature A framework or skeleton of metal or wood inside a statue. Its purpose is to support the statue.

Caliper A jaw-like instrument used to measure the diameter or thickness of an object.

Colossus A giant or colossal statue, much larger than life-size.

Contagious disease A disease that can be spread from person to person.

Copper A reddish-yellow metal that is fairly soft and easy to reshape.

Declaration of Independence The document signed on July 4, 1776, which declared that the United States of America were no longer British colonies.

Forge A fire in which metal is heated until it's soft enough to reshape.

Maquette A scale model of a statue made by the artist. It's used as a guide to making the full-size statue.

Mold (noun) A shape from which additional identical shapes can be made.

Mold (verb) To form something into a particular shape.

Nimbus In art, a halo around the head of a figure.

Ore Rock containing valuable minerals that can be extracted.

Patina A coating that forms naturally on metal as it ages and helps to protect it from corrosion. The patina on copper is bluish-green and is sometimes called **verdigris**.

Pedestal A base on which a statue stands; also called a **plinth**.

Plaster A white powder made from the mineral gypsum. It is combined with water to make a paste used for molding and sculpting.

Plumb line A string with a weight on the end to make it hang vertically. It's used as a guide when measuring.

Pointing up The process of taking measurements from a scale model in order to figure out the size and shape of the actual statue.

Republic A type of government in which the country's leaders are chosen by the people.

Rivet A short metal rod used to fasten two or more pieces of metal together. The ends of the rivet are beaten with a hammer while the rivet is hot. This makes the ends swell outward so the rivet cannot fall out of its hole.

Scaffolding A temporary framework put up around a structure while it is being built.

Seal A metal disk that is used to stamp a medal-like design into a piece of wax. The wax impression can be attached to an official document to show that it is authentic.

Vein A layer of ore found between layers of rock underground.

Index

Gustave Eiffel

Bartholdi was not the only famous figure involved in the construction of the Statue of Liberty. Gustave Eiffel, a French civil engineer and architect, designed the internal iron framework for the statue. However, nowadays Eiffel is better known for the wrought-iron lattice tower he built in Paris: the world-famous Eiffel Tower. The tower was completed in 1889, having been commissioned for the entrance to that year's World's Fair in Paris.

It was initially greeted with a very negative reception by leading French intellectuals, such as the writer Guy de Maupassant, who labeled it as ugly and pointless. Today, it is known and loved worldwide, having become an iconic image of France and a tourist attraction that has been visited by more than 250 million people since its opening.

In addition to his fame as an architect and engineer of landmarks and rail bridges in France, Eiffel has an equally glowing reputation in the field of aerodynamics. After retiring from architecture, he began investigating the air resistance of different surfaces, and built a wind tunnel in 1909 to test the wings used in early aircraft developed by pioneers like the Wright brothers.

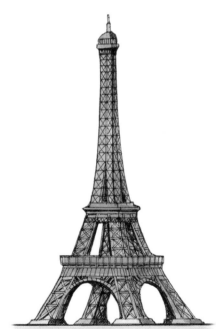

Top U.S. Landmarks

The Lincoln Memorial in Washington, D.C., was built between 1914 and 1922. The statue of Abraham Lincoln sitting and contemplating was carved by the Piccirilli brothers, a well-respected family of marble carvers, and supervised by the popular American sculptor Daniel Chester French. It is 19 feet (5.8 m) tall and made out of 28 blocks of white Georgia marble.

The building housing the statue was designed in the style of a Greek temple by New York architect Henry Bacon. It is 204 feet (62 m) long, 134 feet (41 m) wide, and 99 feet (30 m) tall, and features 36 Doric columns.

It is strongly associated with the civil rights movement, mainly because Martin Luther King Jr. delivered his famous "I Have a Dream" speech to 250,000 people on the memorial grounds.

Mount Rushmore is located in the Black Hills of South Dakota. It is one of the world's largest sculptures, and depicts the faces of four U.S. presidents: George Washington, Thomas Jefferson, Theodore Roosevelt, and Abraham Lincoln.

It was designed by the sculptor Gutzon Borglum, after the idea was dreamed up by a lawyer and writer named Doane Robinson, who was the official historian of South Dakota in 1923.

The sculpture took 15 years to create, although most of this time was taken up with raising the funds. To carve the faces into the granite cliff, workers removed 450,000 tons of rock with explosives, pneumatic drills, and chisels. Each finished face is roughly 60 feet (18 m) high.